Different take 1

A Collection of Poems

Chanchal Nandy

BookLeaf Publishing

India | USA | UK

Made with ❤ on the BookLeaf Publishing Platform
www.bookleafpub.in
www.bookleafpub.com

Dedication

*The Book is dedicated to the fond memories of my departed Father (**Late Narendra Nath Nandy**), Mother (**Late Amiya Rani Nandy**) and two Brothers (**Late Deepak Kumar Nandy** and **Late Aloke Kumar Nandy**). The above four have played a crucial role in the making of what I am today. So my unequivocal dedication must go to them. Below I am narrating, one by one, the decisive roles played by them that have catered to my ongoing deep dive into the aura of dedication.*

My father was an ardent lover of literature. Not only vernacular, he also had a great knowledge of English literature. The niceties, uniqueness and ever-appealing call of English literature had been impregnated in me by him. Being a science student all through, I feel a great passion for English from his inspiration. And bit by bit, I had been drawn to writing in English.

My mother gave me her love, moral support and emotional support amply, which perhaps led me towards my writing spree.

***Late Deepak Kumar Nandy** was a very kind, passionate and concerned elder-most brother. He had enthused me a lot to follow my current journey.*

***Late Aloke Kumar Nandy** was, in fact, instrumental in choosing my career path. In what way can I get success – by judging my capacity and capability – perhaps he had etched the road map of my future trajectory.*

Acknowledgements

I am really thankful to **BookLeaf Publication** and its personnel for the necessary guidance to complete my first Book. I am also indebted to my daughter, **Miss Nishigandha Nandy**, regarding some technical issues arising at the time of its making. Now I will delve into the above two's useful guidance, help and cooperation that made this book see the light.

First, I will mention the contribution of **BookLeaf Publication** to creating my book. Right from the beginning, they have lent their helping hand. Usual tips and tidbits were being shared with me either in email or in WhatsApp on a regular basis. Also, they have a live chat option to clear immediate doubt and confusion from where I got immense help. Their approach was all-through cordial and friendly.

Now I must mention my daughter's contribution. She was on her semester exams and got heavily busy with her study and preparation. Nevertheless, she spent some valuable time completing my book publication project. She had looked after all the technical parts of its making. Otherwise, I would have to take help from outside, which was not so convenient and trustworthy.

Preface

The author right now is on his writing spree and still in the making in the poetry vertical in literature. He is now an employee of a Public Sector Undertaking in India. His book titled 'Different take 1...' contains poems in different verticals. The author gets inspiration from his friends' circle and one of his sisters (**Mrs. Susmita Bose**). He started writing first in various social media, souvenirs and magazines. Now he wants to foray into professional writing. His first book can be looked down upon as a sincere attempt in that direction.

The author of this book can be described as a newcomer. Prior to it, he had no other foray into any publication of repute like **BookLeaf Publication**. Starting with writing first on various social media platforms—such as WhatsApp and Facebook—he has ventured into other segments also. His initial writings pertained to socio-political subjects. Apart from that, the writings had linkages with current affairs, pressing needs and predicaments and problems faced by common people. Writing, at that time, was of text in nature and had been sufficiently lengthened to cover every arising side of particular topics. All the above lengthy English – devoid of vernacular – writing had often led to ridicule and mockery of the author by acquaintances. Then the said author had forayed into the 'Letter to the Editor' section of almost all renowned English dailies in India. Apart from that, he had written in magazines and souvenirs. Then he had forayed into X-handle and blogs. The book 'Different take 1...' is his latest foray with a lot of aspirational dreams.

The book 'Different take 1...' is a collection of poems. The writer has tried his best to transcend his ideas, emotions and perspectives in this book. Also, the writer hasn't stuck to a subject on and on. Instead, he delved into a wide spectrum to give it a different dimension. His journey encompasses nature, love, flora & fauna, fervour, human traits, etc. Containing forty-one poems, the book has been written with care, purpose and integrity. No doubt the bottom line of the book is to give some messages to its readers. The author is here soliciting any kind of suggestion or review or correction to his said book. Last but not the least, the author is expecting a warm response from his readers. Hereby the author is also earnestly appealing to its readers to make it more and more public if being delighted upon by its reading. Definitely then the said book and its author will get their worth undoubtedly.

Sweet Love

Love isn't only a four-letter word
But it signifies a lot more
Whether plausible or imaginary
It must have had some lasting impact on both
minds...

At their tender ages, it's like a spark and instinct
Causing ample opportune to feel the pulses of
opposite sexes
By coming closer or by imaginary portraying
They soaked in all new feelings of affection...

They gradually turned true lovers from mere
friends/acquaintances
A new feeling of liking, faithfulness and
dependability
Cropped up as it moved further and further...

Knowingly or unknowingly a bonding
Being in the making between them
Gradually they become more and more known to
each other
By getting closer bodily, heartily and mind...

On their way, forward journey, they judge each
other threadbare
Bit of empathy, fondness and passion
engulfed both of them
But alas, all such affairs don't see the end of the
light...

Sometimes it goes up to liking each other
Gamut of externalities, such as societal, familial
and circumstantial, doesn't permit it to go
further
But present lovers may become future life
partners also
When the veracity of love and affection subdued
the emerging constraints...

Whether any love affair gets its fruition or not
It can't be dislodged altogether
Because a lasting impression of each other's liking
will be in their walk down the memory lane
forever...

Religion

Is it called religion
When it brings
Only enmity and grudges among people
Instead of brotherhood...

True religion
Is altogether different from the above
It speaks volumes
Of mutual coexistence...

Here humanity comes first
Along with compassion and trust
Where intra- or inter-bickering
Is few and far between...

People here think of
Inclusion rather than exclusion
Devoid of selective concern
It entails a broader spectrum of masses...

In the name of religion
Any bigotry or intolerance is unwarranted
By and large, religions are meant for people to be
wholesome
So it can't be the differentiator at any cost...

You Are There So

You are there so
Man indulges in activities
That can fulfil your wish
Or wanting to some extent...

But your demand
Unlikely to be a restricted one
Keeps going and going
From the smaller one to the bigger...

Many, often, men want to please you
To his best effort, capability and offering
Which may not be your deserving one
Yet man is on his own way to fulfilment...

Many stunning creatures in our world
Have connections with your lasting memory
Sometimes you become the cause of perils also
Yet you are the catapult of proceedings
nonetheless...

Time – thou harsher yet inescapable

Time flows like
A vibrant and meandering river
Without having any time per se
To roll back and revisit...

Though we may call you
Selfish, inconsiderate and crude
Yet from your own perspective
You have impeccably stayed put...

You are like a staunch eavesdropper
Witnessing a gamut of activities
Relentlessly at your disposal
As a bystander of colossal integrity...

Your pedagogy of a mass all through
An exposé of reality in different times
From a vast depository of good and evil
Can't be ruled out but to be admitted
nonetheless...

Bhul-Bhulia

Is it a curse?
Or a blessing in disguise
I think both ways can be feasible
As per the ground situation per se...

Sometimes it helps us
Doing away with our
Agony, tension and overthinking
By becoming oblivious altogether...

There is a heresy that
Forgetfulness of them
Being compensated by their intelligence
But it's not always falling in line as predicted
above...

Anyway their forgetfulness
Be it trivial or significant in nature
Wreaked havoc sometimes
To the extent of unbecoming and thorny...

But the above fault lines
Has had an ingress to all and sundry
Of different magnitude, façade and trait
Making life hilarious, hazardous and miserable...

On A Winter Day

Winter – you are
Something different, really
Apart from your chill
You have had other noticeable features also...

Though in a tropical country like us
You seem to be the odd man out
Yet your brief presence
In a calendar year...

Definitely is a game changer
Your presence fills us
What is cold all about
In the aplenty hot, humid and perspiration...

Your homecoming just after a long gap
Soothing and comforting initially
So as also at the fag end of your departure
But your crescendo is bothering a bit...

Your advent makes us heavier by apparel
We become a bit clumsy, confined and restricted
But our tastes get variance with your produce
And your seasonal flowers definitely attract our
beholding...

Comforting weather at your short spell
Give us extra vigour and workability
Which often leads to our outings, gatherings for
causes and celebrating occasions
We can't tolerate your absence and hope your
presence in your own way...

A Tiny Lush Green

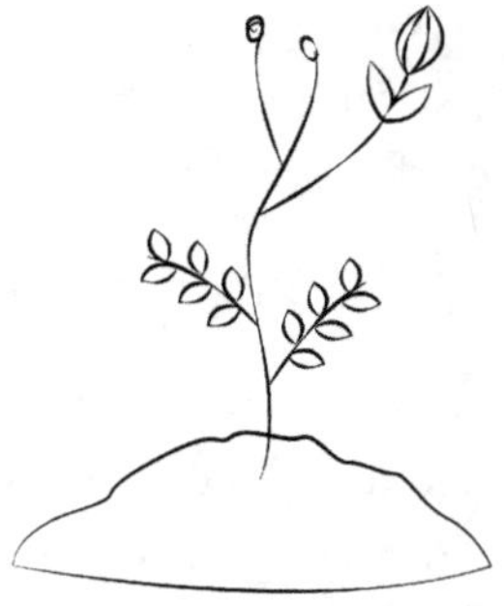

You are the few and far between
Amidst the aplenty concrete
A dichotomy nonetheless
Yet you are in a continuing fight...

Your roadside existence
As a cynosure of beauties
Can't be ignored in the first place
For me, you are also an eye-catcher...

As if you have made your landscape
A green pasture ignoring the peripheral
Awkwardness of brick-and-mortar
Your pristine beauty at the fag end of the rainy
season
Has become a template of extraordinaire...

Your embellishment on your own way
Without any touch of artificial makeover
Has definitely given you a façade
Of your own as an unmatched entity...

Suddenly you have become an object
Of grasping as early as possible
By the land sharks in and around
Alas, nobody has come to your rescue...

Once an attraction of passersby and onlookers
You sooner will go to the oblivion
By losing your entity altogether
Once and for all, we will forfeit your mesmerising
beauty in the vicinity...

The Rising Sun

You are so fascinating
Each and every day usually appearing
Anew with different mesmerising look
You never become boring to the onlookers.

Except for those, some odd days
Being subdued by clouds or eclipses

By your magic wand
Often creates a bit of hallucination
Which we sincerely deserved
To get away from repeat continuation

We get bemused and bewildered
Right from your uprising
From horizon to go above step by step
Your variety in colour, shape and brightness

At different levels and states
Always become seeing is unbelieving
Transition of your colour in a rapid gap
From reddish – saffron – yellow to silvery canvas

You become warmer with each passing phase
Meanwhile, change in shape also occurring
Versatility, thy name is you
Always appeared to us with a gamut of view

In one way, you are the main source of all energy
Deciphering it in your solar system abounds.
Never think of self and well-being.
You decay relentlessly your valuable fuel

For day in and out, billions of years
In exchange, you have never been wanting
Thus, you appeared in a mood of disbursal
Keeping away from getting all sorts of favours

Scarcely your response to subjected atrocities
Being meted out to your entire system
Manifested as a storm-like outburst
Your such endurance is nothing but godliness

By dint of which you are being so proactive
And being treated with godly awe and respect
We depend on you indispensably for survival
Then you have had a need of per se revival

Your shining gives darkness a meaning
Otherwise, it may become nightmarish
We all owe you a lot
Can't deny you anyway at last...

Go Ahead

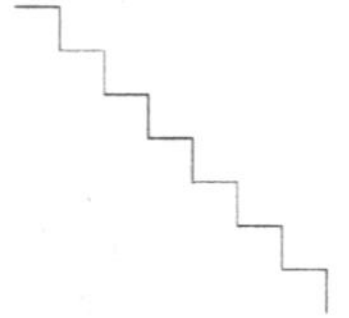

Life is full of struggles
Whatever background you have had
Or resources abound
You can't but escape...

The hardest reality
Of arduous journey
Through which you can
Get settled in any profession...

Either by your own choice
Or by cherry-picking
Sometimes you may get influenced also
By surrounding to decide your path of journey...

Whatever be it for you
You have to continue on your path
With utmost sincerity, integrity and passion
So go ahead with your journey till it gets some
efficacy and conclusion...

Midas Tough

Nature can play a miracle
Anytime and any moment
Unusual hit trail of mid-March of a year
Can be done away with all of a sudden rains...

This anticlimax is quite surprising
But it can't be unpredictable either
And can be foretold beforehand
With our advancement in science and
technology...

Yet how it will unfurl till the end
As an aftereffect of its footfall
Can't be foretold precisely
Here whims of nature...

Prevailed over any anticipation
With its magical touch
It can indulge altogether a different aura
Which can be plausible in the first place...

The change from summer-like fervour
To its volte-face pro-winter fervour
With the buttress of rain and chilling wind
Has given the taste of chilling once again...

Thus nature can change its façade
and manifestation abrupt
On its very own way
Causing topsy-turvy in its weather pattern
Which can entail refreshing variation also...

Alluring Ocean

You are truly a live canvas of vastness, variety and
beauty
Before your enormous contour
Everything nearby
Appeared to be...

Minute and minuscule
Yet you are so humble and magnanimous
And never being boastful of
Your gigantic and monstrous existence...

We learn giving from you
Your returning back every item
Whichever is being thrown or sunk or immersed
Is an exemplary template of a spendthrift...

You are the livelihood of numerous people
One way or another
Feeding flora and fauna in your captivity
Yourself become a buttress for sustainability...

Navigation through you
Has had ample scope and facilities
You act as a sensible connector
Between two landmasses, countries and even
continents...

Being a template of beauty
You also make others beautiful by your vicinity
Such as the navigation of the Sun, clouds and
other creatures and the glittering of the skyline at
night
Upon you or crisscrossing you...

Your to-and-fro ricochetting waves
Etching marks on the shore
As a unique sculpted pattern
Your silvery fluorescence sand particles on the
shore get twinkled by falling sunshine...
You have ever been fascinating to us
All through the generations in an infinite time
cycle...

Rustic Beauty

Not being usually seen
When is being seen then
You are quite awe-making
By your harsher reality rather than some
makeover one...

This happened while I was on a journey
On a bus from the metro city Kolkata
To a far away hamlet
Is it like an unexpecting or happening by chance...

The gal wasn't a
Known copybook beauty
Of fair complexion
But quite contrary to it...

Being darker in skin colour
She was an eye-catcher
By her sharp, distinct and unique appearance
Her hair was thick, vantablack and deeply
concentrated stuff...

A radiant glow was emanating
From her sparkling face to scatter in and around
Without any makeup or refurbishing
Here her originality superseded any artificial
cosmetic makeovers...

The gal was strongly built
With a standard height
Devoid of any wrinkles or untoning in the skin
Her curvatures and sculptures all through were
worth attracting...

It is her perfect and unadulterated rustic beauty
Which have had to be reckoned with
unquestionably
Whatever might be the way of looking

Her simplistic beauty, along with a humble
appearance, gave her the unique feature...

Inherent inside when gets reflected outside
Quite naturally and spontaneously
Then definitely it supersedes
It's only starkly showing the exterior...

Welcome, New Year!

Year after year you return
And the older version retreats
The newer one lays its footprint...

As if with an all-new vigour and enthu
Everything gets started afresh
After bidding adieu to the past one...

The eternal game of these departing and
launching years
Existed early, now also continuing and will
continue forever
The none but years per se witnessing its trajectory
on and on...

In our short lifespan
We ourselves get entwined with the few
proceedings by self
Know the past from our predecessor...

But in our non-existence in the abode
Future will remain as unknown
Where we are quite helpless...

We can only guess about the coming future
From the perspective of the present ongoing
But it will be blind anticipation rather than a
reality...

But only future
Will tell the future
Which will be revealed to our successor only...

Year at your afresh relaunch
Obviously we get a knee-jerk reaction
That ostensibly will come as an instinct of
changer...

We get decorated with new clothes
Surrounding will also get a makeover along with
it
We will get reverberated by the new wave of
change...

As if we will get swayed
Into the paradigm of newness
Where we get oblivious to our sorrow and
suffering for the time being...

Probably this jolt and spark
Of the new year is a great repository and impulse
for us
Which we enjoy a lot, although for a short while...

Because of that
We have had a humble request to you
Year after year, you please come to our Earth...

Totally in a different new look
By pushing aside the pale, tottered and lacking
liveliness...

Although for some short while at the very onset
of the new year
We get inundated with ecstasy and hope
At your very spectacular new homecoming...

Morning Sky Also Can Be The Eye Catcher

Beauty of nature is unlimited
Can be exposed anywhere and anytime
We need just watching eyes and heartily feeling
Then the divulging of beauty is assured...

Recently I have had such an experience
Even morning sky with fully blown sun
May create a distinction
If being watched upon vividly and minutely...

Sunrise in a clear sky
Definitely is a pristine beauty
Be it emerging from the sea or back of hills
We get bemused at its look on the horizon...

In the former, the sky was decorated
By clouds with a special pattern
Faraway from the sun, it was bit scattered
At the closest, it was consolidated mostly...

Also variation in colours in the sky canvas
Creates some mesmerising looks unexpectedly
As if some artists of par excellence
Have painted the sky canvas immaculately...

Clouds far far away were reddish-golden
With the juxtaposition of grey ones
Whereas nearer to the sun
It was golden with blackish attachment...

Closer to the sun
Light beams were emerging like many focuses
Piercing the layers of clouds
Seeing was unbelieving and haunting at its best...

Alas, If We Were Reborn

In the unfathomable time frame
Our life is minuscule
It comes and passes by
Like a glimpse...

From our infancy
To childhood
Time goes by
Like a vibrant and fierce flow of rivers...

Before we comprehend it
Totally or stepwise
The transition of our most enjoyable time
Takes a breakneck speed...

Sooner we enter into our teenage era
We start dreaming
To become what we want in the future
Either we crack or get deflected...

In our life
We get either settled on a firm landing
And keep on continuing
Or have a roller coaster ride...

Ultimately, one way or another
Most of us can dock
Successfully to our earnings' launchpad
With self-help or others' support...

But we keep on dreaming
One materialises, another in the offing
Our wanting, expectation and aspiration
Never dried up totally...

Only its traits, levels and scopes
Changes with the time
But it can't be exhausted anyway

We hope against our hopes repeatedly...

At last, our life comes to an end
But our many dreams remain unfulfilled
In the end, we lament
For our scarce time at hand...

Had it been more longer
Then we probably get some more completions
Alas, it can't be possible
So we stay put on our reborn desperately...

So that unfinished doable
Can get completed
This repeated cycle of born and urge to be reborn
Keep continuing in the realm of eternal time
cycle...

Exploring Beauty

Unraveling beauty
Has no ending
If it exposes one way
Then other ways get opened...

Isn't it a forever mystery
That enthrals us time and again
And haunts us all the way
Awaiting stealthily to be unearthed...

Cropping up everywhere in different facade
And encompassing land, water and skyline
You are spectacular in every way
Can't it be ignored, come what may

We never escape from your serenity
Your appeal ever alluring
Leads to our running after you
Thus, our nearing with you gets entwined...

Our Memorable Journey

At last, our journey ended
Days were just passed by
Like turning of pages
Devoid of grasping it in its entirety...

As if all those days
Begun to end so abruptly
We couldn't help but willy-nilly
Being compelled to oversee your relentless flow...

Alas, if it could have been slower
Then we can enjoy it a bit more
But time always comes and passes
On its own way...

Especially for our rejoicing moment
Time flows with a rapid stride
Whereas bad times always
Passes at a snail's speed

Together we have gone for outing
For our refreshment and rejuvenation
The veritable localities and scenic beauty were
added to that
Heartily we get soaked in the fervour irresistibly.

But our returning from journey
Looking a bit morose
We will now be backed to
Our usual chores...

Our momentary dreaming sojourn
Abruptly got its conclusion
But left definitely an indelible etch into our mind
Now awaiting another one to dislodge us even
more...

Mystery, Thy Name Is You

You are truly
Ever mysterious
Sometimes you are plausible
Otherwise untenable mostly...

Often you become an inspiration
For our way forwarding
Also appears sometimes as doomsday
To retract us from our rejoicing trajectory...

Your galvanising face
Often sparkle to amuse us
While your morose one
Disheartens us a lot...

Your gladness and cheer
Mostly lead to our fulfilment
Whereas your unpleasant
Make us worrysome...

Your passion and delicacy
Are worthy of cherishing
On the other hand, your anger
Causes awe and apprehension...

You often appeared as a beckon
That leads us towards prosperity
Whereas your unscrupulous charting
Often leads to our crestfallen...

Sometimes what you speak out
Isn't a true reflection of your mind
Whereas your not-spoken words
Is the true urge of your innermost...

So you were/are/would be uncanny
And man will ever quest for you
But you couldn't be busted ever
And will remain mysterious ever...

Flock Of Birds

Many often living creatures
Like flock of birds
Even on a communication tower nearby
Create an aura of surprise and splendour

Recently I have had an opportunity
To behold something like that
From my habitat
The said tower was encircled by big trees...

Birds were roaming in and around
By following a definite pattern
Afternoon sun was glowing
At its low ebb at the skyscape then...

Sitting atop the trees
Some birds were getting ready
To fly at a higher reach of the tower
Sooner some get landed on it...

They start climbing upward
From initial landing position
To the extreme upper reach of the tower
By gradually ascending...

Then they follow
Back to square one journey
To land on top of the trees
And thus completing one cycle of trajectory

Other sections of birds
Do follow the same cycle
The rhythm of this getting on/off
Was sequential to bring ergonomy and synergy

Flight from trees to tower and vice versa
Was so organised and disciplined
That no swarming of birds
Being taken place either atop trees or all along the
tower...

The entire episode of birds' journey
Has created an illusion and dilemma
Seeing was unbelieving for me
Yet what had been seen by me was a reality by all
terms...

What They Want

Definitely, it's a big billion question
Which haunted us
Time immemorial...

But no definite conclusion
Whatsoever being emerges
Before, now or even after time – colossal...

Sometimes even it is left to God
As a last resort
When all conjectures dried up
Even God being ended up without any clue...

Without having inside out most of the time
They have become a perpetual enigma to be
busted
Men are always on the quest to unearth it
But being woefully faded up, they finally give it
up for good...

This forever mystery has no answer
As because its exclusive stakeholders
Women themselves have been emptied
Of having any definite, discreet, clear-cut
deserving...

Their wanting is topsy-turvy forever.
Going here and there by multiple reflectors
Like some fictitious mirages appearing here and
yond
On the street of a summer-day noon...

Will this unknown ever be busted
Or being remained unresolved forever
To make us ever perplexed
In its labyrinth year after year...

The tug of war between their wanting and
unwanting
Along with a roller coaster ride of priority

It can be assumed that for women, men are simply executors
Of their ensuing demand or dislodging something thereof...
They deserve men shouldn't meddle apart from that

Bygone Childhood...

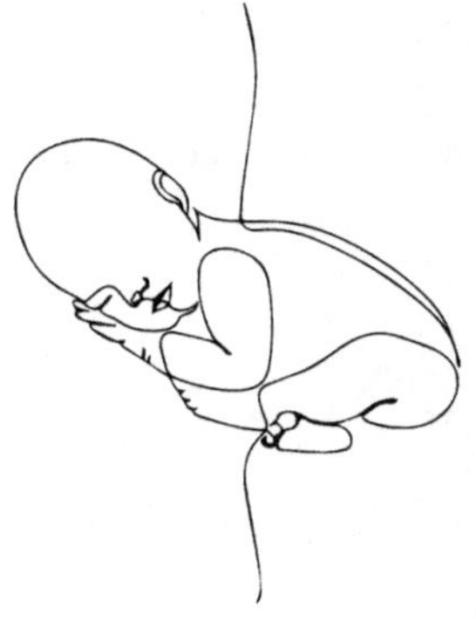

Alas, childhood will not return
Only sweet memories of it
Ricochetting off and on
Momentarily it swayed us

To a different realm
Suddenly we become younger in mind
Though physically may not be so
To achieve the same agility as yesteryear

But a momentary flash of memory in mind
Leads to vigorous stirring inside
By a flicker, we get back into
The very old, sweet memory

Virtually and unknowingly
We land in a new fiefdom
By setting aside our present aura
And gladly take a deep dive into yesteryear's
childhood

All of a sudden our age
Take a reverse journey
From older ones we get younger
Virtually rather than in reality
This transition takes place all of a sudden
As a fallout, childhood again revisited
Alas, at our very childhood
We can't cherish it to the fullest

Owing to not comprehending its gravitas fully
We misjudged it and couldn't follow its trajectory.
Childhood's limitation haunted us a bit
Be it in finance, decision-making and freedom

Then we aspire to spend it
As quickly as possible
Ignoring its aplenty treasure trove
Charm, variety and uniqueness

With our getting older
Our childhood left afar
But now we can evaluate those in totality

Being mature enough it helps us to do so

By introspection, goodies of childhood
Get exposed to us now
Which isn't being widely uncovered then
Maturity has definitely given us this acumen

Younger age is full of tension
Cut-throat competition, agony and disquiet
With an increase in complexity
Relentless rejoicing is a far cry

On the other hand
Childhood is brimmed with
Simplicity, liveliness, charm and passion
Not flooded with tension, agony and ire

The childhood is really cherishing and rejoicing
It can't stay forever or long lasting
We have had compulsion
To let it go one day

With a dejected and disheartened heart
Here can lament at best but no reverting
whatsoever
Childhood must begin to end one day
Yet those spectacular days will be in our sweet
repository...

Sad Demise...

Any lovely creature
Be it big or small
Around yourself
May move you a bit...

Especially tiny creatures like kittens
Can be the cause of profound grief
Here I will tell a tale of two kittens
Small enough yet passionate to love...

They were being beheld nearby
And were siblings in relation also
You may or may not like cats
But their kittens are really appealing...

Because of their agility and
Innocence up to the brim
They were roaming all around
To my courtyard and adjacent area...

One was hued by spotty black
With the majority of whitish pigmentation
Another was spotted by yellow
On its comparative white dominance...

Their movement by following the mother cat
As a tiny apprentice
And playing between them or with their mother
Was definitely a reminiscence of our childhood...

Watching their movement and restlessness
Was really alluring and enjoyable
I think it will touch everyone's heart
Irrespective of their tenderness or toughness...

Their fearless napping and resting
And soaking up the sun in a chill
And trembling roams at sudden rise from asleep
Was really touchy, tendering and hallucinating...

Alas, all of a sudden
The yellow-spotted kitten succumbed
Making all of us disheartened and shocked
By dying, the little kitten has proved its worth to
be lamented upon...

Angst Of Theirs And Ours...

Females are humble or delicate usually
Yet they may be firebrand and aggressive
When being subjected to prolonged provocation
and oppression
Their outburst then is a template of severity and
concern...

Probably their pent-up anger
Along with grievance by and large
Being simmered inside them for long...
Can be the outburst of an impromptu explosion

Whether we agree or not
Rage/anger manifestation
Of women and men are different
Men's angst and thereby repercussions are usually
quick vis-à-vis women...

As a natural fallout, men's cooldown
Supposedly being, takes less time
Than women's counterpart
All above played here as a leveller, somehow in
disguise...

Ultimately this episode of
Anger and cool down of men and women
Goes on continuing till it is absorbed by both
In the end, rapproachment superseded
whodunit...

Rain, Are You Far Away...

When the Earth is scorching
Environment being dried up
And make us forced to feel
What extreme summer looks like...

Rain your blessings
We are deserving...
The unprecedented summer this year
Changed all dynamics

Instead of usual hotter days
We are facing your sternest rage this time...
Now the rain can only
Give us the respite...

Here, rare heat has become the new normal
As if after a long gap
Nature itself tests our
Tolerance, resilience and bearing...

We have had done
Lots of experiments, exploitations and harakiri on
nature...
Now time has come for her
To revert it by our own coin

Here we are quite helpless
Rather encountering it, we have to bear with her
music...
But any benevolence of nature is a short-stint
memory
For human beings conspicuously...

Only inconveniences make us feel the ferocity of
nature
Otherwise, we are quite indifferent to her
Having been nurtured by her day in, day out
We really become ungrateful, selfish and
impudent to her even under aegis also...

What a fallacy and dilemma!
Alas, all those inflicted perils are being made at
our very own behest

Doing Late Or Being Belated Ones...

More or less
We have had faced this agony
In our spectrum of life cycles
Whether we are being punctual or not...

For tardy individuals
Doing late is common
Whereas for punctual ones
It can be evolved from uncontrolled
externalities...

Devoid of self-inflicted delay
They are being tagged as belated
Whereas belated fellows on few occasions
Happen to achieve the 'punctual' tag by chance...

It appears to them
Like rain, even before any cloud formation
Thus they get an unexpected leveraging in
valuable time-domain
Make them elated, boastful and brimmed with
high morale...

In the parameters of tardiness's increasing
propensity
We have had rare, occasional and habitual
contenders
Alas, instead of transitioning from more to less
frequencies of delay
Most get swayed by its surging...

Being belated causes anxiety, ire and less
confidence
Not only for the doers per se
But also to other associated individuals
Like an endemic's gradual spillover...

Whereas a scheduled person faced this music
quite the opposite
By portraying themselves as an exemplary
template of punctuality
They induced others to follow suit
Here they become conduits of goodies genuinely...

But no one wants to tag the ignominy of belated
ones
Punctuality makes life decent, coordinated and
disciplined
And everyone tries to imbibe it one way or
another.
Come what may, the above endeavour goes on
continuing

Expenditure And Affordability Sometimes Become Ultra Vires Also...

In our life cycle
We have to face awkwardness
And dilemma
It's a part of life...

Everyone has to encounter it
Irrespective of affordability
It comes all of a sudden
To all and sundry...

It's beyond any pre-assumption
How the coming days
Going to pass by
Can't be predicated or guessed always...

Even having money with you
You can't expend as needed
Some prominence of priority
Will dislodge your immediate plan...

I have had a recent experience of it
On the fag end of a particular month
When I have had a compulsion to run
On a shoestring budget...

Then some unexpected new expenditure
Being cropped up to daunt me badly
Which I have to face invariably without dodging
And led to my crippling financially on that very
month...

You may have less money in captivity
But it doesn't guarantee any lesser expenditure
It's beyond our control and being guided by
exigency
Even expenditure gets leapfrogged from unwanted
doables...
Which we want to avoid...

Otherwise, everything goes in disarray
And might be the cause of taking credit
Whose hangover will go next month, definitely
Some compromise of needs then be a better one...

Many Facades Of Love...

(The poem is a commemoration of recently passed Valentine's Day or Lovers' Day. But love can't be restricted to a special day. It is universal and intertwined with every possible life)

Love is more of a feeling
Than being seen or exhibited
It has enormous facades
Of which each one has a specific trait...

It is as deep as ocean
As delicate as petals
Soft and galvanising as of morning dew
Enormously vast as the atop sky...

Its spread is perhaps unlimited
Can't it be shackled anyway
Not being limited by distance
Love is all-pervasive, be it nearby or faraway...

Love relates to care and affection
Between mother and her child
In friendship, love is exposed as a reliability
While in siblings, it is mingling...

For true and passionate lovers
Love resonates heart to heart
Mind to mind
And for divine ones, even soul to soul...

Love is a true conduit
Bridging the gap and differences relentlessly
Despite our gamut of exclusivity
We come closer through love...

Devoid of love, relationship can't exist
It's like an unseen connecting string
Joining us holistically as a big entity
Across the world from time immemorial...

Sweet Birthday...

You come every year
Like a stunning harbinger
To make it a memorable one
Usually the D-day's before and after...

No way it's always a celebration day
Overwhelming us momentarily, what may
Yet its presence
Felt by us all together...

Definitely, it gives us an impetus
Which can only be irresistible whatsoever
That plunges us into the realms
Of charm, delight and enjoyment...

Along with insisting us to go down
The memory lane's
Farthest extension of remembering
Where we can reminisce the sparkling moments
extensively...

Thou Name Is Festivity...

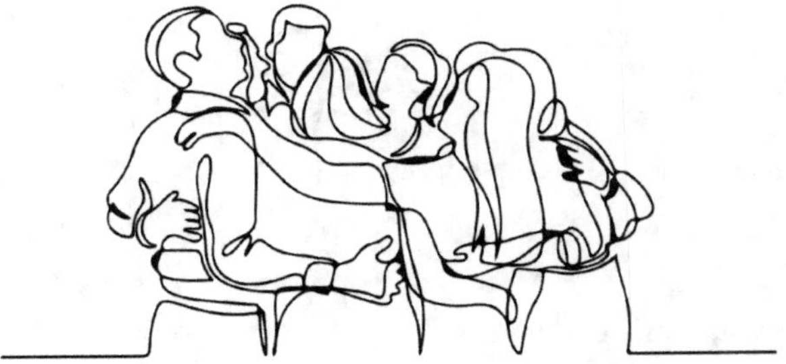

You came
As like a gale
To refresh us amidst abound pale and gloom
Thus bring a smile for a while...

Yet your launching for us
The most fascinating one
And you get embossed with your inherent
rejoicing
At which we soaked ourselves in abundance
And get lost mostly to your feel-good aura...

Your presence definitely makes the difference
And pursued us to do away with the crippling
grievances
Being indifferent to our suffering a bit
We ventured out to taste the impulse of
rejuvenation...

Your magic touch
Often makes the ambiance flourish
You are in your turn a great appetiser
Ready to instill your fervour and gaiety...

Fresh, Fresher...

Recently I had come across the same forest
Which was very well known to me...

So far, crisscrossing its spread and round trip
Have had no noticeable impact on me
Previous glances at it appear nothing anew...

With strewn deadwood here and there
Piercing sunshine's befalling at its ground
Was scattered by design, owning to its porous
canopy
Chattering of birds was renting the air
And the insects were roaming within with their
signature sounds
This was the usual feature of most parts of the
years...

But my visit to it on a peak monsoon day
Was totally different in variable yardsticks
The changes in its outlook had a bearing on my
perspective also
Surprisingly it was the same creation of nature
with two different facades

These glaring differences were being covertly and
overtly noticeable
Sometimes seeing is boring and monotonous
While seeing is unbelieving on few occasions also

This time (my rainy day visit), the forest was
embellished by its own
In totality, on every possible front...

With its dense canopy of aplenty greenery
That was restricting the sunshine's befalling
almost to a naught
The floor of the forest had metaphored into
A vast greenery of carpet having almost no
breakages

As if a mystical, mist-like aura
Hold sway the ambiance overwhelmingly

The totality of its perfection in every vertical
Have had a definite resemblance
With a fully grown-up, well-built person's
Ulterior development in every front of physique

As if vibes of bliss emanating from this forest
Signifies its hearty fulfilment in every vertical

Freshly embellished, the forest was beaming
To its brim at the passionate touch of rain
Resembling a newly-wed bridegroom's
Radiant bliss, fulfilment and ecstasy in the aura of
her
Better half's passion, empathy and liking...

Long Absence...

Absence evokes detachment...
It's the harshest truth
That long absence
From any engagement or involvement
Feel the pangs of discontinuation...

Whether we admit it or not
Absence from routine activities
Always creates void
Knowingly or unknowingly...

Be it in a group or team or among acquaintances
Any breakup of continuance
Feels its need the most
Whereas continuance is a flow of life...

Where we don't feel any abruptions
As if all are gliding
Our days are just passing away
With this, our spent time also has had a smooth
ride...

It's like a steady flow of consistent river
Being embedded with specific bits and rhythm
Making the journey a confluence of sorts
Almost undettered and unaffected...

What a dilemma!
Long presence feels no difference
Whereas any absence
Make the difference...

Absence creates concern and fonding
From the very emotive mind
Albeit of practicality
It's a spontaneity from the depths of the
innermost...

Isn't it beyond explanation
As per usual logic, cause and effect
Our feelings and vibes
Not follow a definite pattern...

Can't we deny it at any cost
It's a music of life
None has had any escaping
From it whatsoever...

Hope Elusive – Not So...

In the parlance
Of cloud of no way
There's always galvanising hope
Knocking at your corridor
It is to be unearthed and deciphered...

Otherwise, a despondency
May looms large
To grab our all potential and effort
To its nadir of irreversibility...

Hope is like a fuel
To our continuous journey
It can get exhausted sometimes
From a major setback or drubbing...

But to drag our life further
Some new hope has to be resurfaced
Or may be replenished accordingly...

Dejection can't give us impetus
Rather, it has a bit of domino effect
Spreading from one arena to other
Debilitating any hope whatsoever...

Stay tuned to hope at its best
Or at least ascribe hoping against hope
So that our journey
Get the needed exuberance of way forwarding...

And Keep Going With Hope As Much As You Can...

Hope can advent anew if we deserve so
Which can lead to some exalted exuberance
Resulting in our vibrancy and proactivity...

In reality, hope can't have a stopover
For a positive mind, it has no halt.
Rather, it has a journey
Of going on and on...

For a negative mind
It can have multiple stopovers
Or it's altogether jettisoning
Two antitheses above are nothing but a
Reflection of our way of thinking

Any disheartened fellow
Has to bear the pangs of it undoubtedly
But s/he can turn around anytime if wishes
In the domain of hopefulness
With the strongest determination...

Any hope can get its final outcome
Either in its fructification or failure
But hoping shouldn't have a cessation
Until we breathe our last...

Walk Down The Memory Lane On A Foggy Morning...

The foggy morning that day
Was by far the most denser one
As usually being seen in our plain land...

Of course, its version in hilly areas
Superseded our plain-landed above replica
Yet we can't ignore its severity
Having a closed-quarters linkage with us...

Severe density of it has made the
Visibility in and around to become haywire
Even it miserably failed in handshaking distance
Everything appeared a bit different...

I was on the ride towards my destination
Only the faded light of vehicles was flushing
across
And was being seen from nearer or afar
People on bicycles or on their walks
Being devoid of any emitting sources of light
Appeared like a phantom or shadow from afar...

In this grandiose mystical ambience
The series of buildings and trees were
Completely submerged in the sea of fog
Perhaps heavy downpours can't give them
The above sense of drenching in totality
In fact, everything in its vicinity got soaked a bit...

All those magical moments being seen by us
Is a fallout of fog's coming into being suddenly
But its embedded perils with ecstatic beauties
Can't be mixed up and are to be judged separately
Fog never fosters speed but solicits any slower
movement
Otherwise, we can't soak in its inherent beauties
And the onlookers on the move put their lives in
danger...

Bid adieu...

Any workplace should have
Look-alike as a second home
As we spend there a considerable timespan of our
life...

But everyone hasn't been lucky enough
To get livelihood near home
Or staying at the same place till retirement
Some have to go away or change location
repeatedly...

Today's workplace isn't a cakewalk for anyone
Gradually, it's becoming more and more
Competitive, aspirational and tougher one
A topsy-turvy battle to supersede one by another
in the so-called success ladder
It often entails insidious manoeuvring also
Devoid of merit, vision and excellence as being
deserved
Alas, it's a different ball game altogether in the
professional workspace...

But the retirement of someone throws a different
aura
Here the ensuing retiree and his/her 'biding adieu'
givers (colleagues or bosses)
Discarding the faults/flaws/bitterness whatsoever
get engaged
In exchanging pleasantries, niceties and best
wishes
After all, one of us is leaving the workplace de
facto once and for all
Here we get swayed by intense emotion,
sentiment and pangs of feeling the absence of
someone for good...

Thus for someone, a curtain falls on his/her work
life
With that, so many years' dissatisfaction,
victimhood and injustice
Mostly go under the carpet bereft of any
face-to-face confrontation
Only the sweet old memories
Will ricochet at the vast podium of the memory
realm
Leading to a knee-jerk for thinking differently...
Isn't a spectacular 'bid adieu' then what?

Simmering Motherhood...

Has every female being born with it,
The undercurrent of motherhood?
Most probably, aye, as my observation
Pertaining to close-quarters monitoring at home...

Though it is hard to be off-beat
Yet in de facto, it can be a reality
Female by birth is kind, passionate and sensitive
God has also bestowed on them ample caring and
adjustment prowess...

That is why an undercurrent of motherhood has
Always being flown through them
Even before their procreation of offspring

Making a landfall on them silently

Motherhood can be incipient or vivid
In different vibes and exposition
Yet something must have been there in females
At different stages – be it childhood, teenage,
adolescence and even adulthood...

My daughter, still in her adulthood
Treats her 5-6 dolls (replicas of animals) as her
children
She often observes them, loves them and cares for
them
They stay with her all the time except nature's
calls and she going outside

She is in her sleep and surrounded by them
Having been lucky enough to stay inside her
blanket in winter
And at the same comfort at which she spends her
summers
She often asks queries to them and
Utters the probable answer of them by herself
solely
When anyone hides any of her dolls, she becomes
furious and loses her cool
She kisses, hugs and roams with them, holding
firmly on her lap...

Being at her adulthood and maturity and
happening to be a college goer
When we ask her about all those odd activities
She simply smiles and utters that they're all her
own children...

You can cite it as natural or unnatural
Yet many of her contemporaries – falling into the
same gender as she is
More or less carrying the same ethos and fervour
of motherhood
To a different extent, expose and trait...

Can't we call it a simmering motherhood
Inside any age bracket of femalehood

The Ever-Fascinating Moon...

Probably the moon is our
First gateway to the outer world
Be it child or old, it's ever-appealing
Can't be denied or ignored at any cost...

The restlessness and tantrums of a child
Are often being suppressed by mother
By showing the alluring moon to her kids
The child gets bemused and deflected from the
pathway of angst...

Sometimes our beloved moon helps us
To feed our reluctant children into the lap of
mother
For them, the moon is worthy of immense
watching
The scintillating moon in the night sky
Creating an all-new aura for them
This out-of-world spectacular scenery
Always appears to them as surprising and
enchanting...

But its appeal is unequivocal and inescapable
Transcending the age barrier, generation and
localities
It often changes its hue, shape and look
Which provoked us to at least glance at it at our
opportune time...
It's soothing and comforting mild glow
Irresistibly has become a cynosure of attraction
Even we get detached from our earthly
connections
By a flicker at its hallucinating clarion call...

Our beloved moon, please be kind enough
To mesmerise us day in and day out
Like you have been from colossal times
And up your mesmerising journey forever...

Multi-Tasker Or Having Dexterity...

Frankly speaking, I have had no fascination with
any gender
But I always pay due diligence to the brownie
points of any gender, be it male or female
Here, I am too much open-ended in reviewing...

Himself being a man and lone bread earner
I can't ignore the versatile role being played
By my better half, day in and day out
Usually not being so highlighted because of its
occlusive nature
Her role in our family's upkeep is stupendous...

She has had the arduous task of feeding us
properly
Right from morning hours to our going to bed at
night
Here she provides tiffin, snacks and meals as per
the individualistic or common preferences
Within a permissible time frame all year long...

With that, she has to program well to cope with
the unhindered and timely college-going of her
daughter as well as husband's reaching workplace
She has to have a look after their tiffin, water and
meal prior to departure outside...

She has also to execute household chores regularly
And has to become proactive to monitor
Health, well-being and needs of every member.
For seniors, she has to become extra cautious
Of their nutrient-rich food, proper sleeping and
medication...

With that, she has to delve into the terrain
Of household needs – be it vegetables, groceries,
fruits, apparel, et al.
So that anything doesn't go out of stock
At its sought-after exigencies at a particular point
in time...

Overall, she has been playing the most important
Role of a fulcrum in a family continuously,
Having held the reins of the family's
Wayforwarding under the aegis of her maximum
involvement,
She can be instrumental in upkeeping peace and
tranquillity in the family
By her sheer sacrifice, responsibility and passion...

Will she not be coined as a multi-tasker or
Dexterous judging her by all the above versatile
activities?
Perhaps the Almighty has bestowed on her or
peers
Ample care, patience and adaptability
Someway, it can be routine work on a daily basis
Yet its vast spectrum of differentials can't be
ignored either
If not the above acknowledgement is being
admitted, then we
Definitely fall into the bracket of misogynistic
outlook...

Having A Look At Belle And Getting Dislodged...

Can't we ignore it
Perhaps not possible anyway
Even someone practicing celibacy
May not be resolute enough
To avoid at least a skewed look at a belle...

You may think it not so sober and appropriate
Yet inherent, unstoppable inhibitions of a man
Must drag him towards a glance at her
Either face-to-face or sideways or from whatever
angle is possible...

Men's all-through attraction and liking for them
From time immemorial till date
Has become de facto irresistible and inescapable
But no way it can be treated as belligerent and
uncalled for

In fact, it's a natural instinct of theirs
To get moved vociferously by the slightest glimpse
of a belle
At what angle and perspective it might be
For different individuals, this intense look can be
specific and discreet

Also, the different belles have had different
Expectations to be looked down upon by a guy
She may not have ease or enjoy it
Yet can't discard this lovable and innocent look
altogether...

She has had the constraints to reciprocate
Under the aegis of societal Lakshmanrekha
Yet she will definitely appreciate any decent and
lovable look on her
Here onlookers can momentarily get distracted
From their immediate past state of mind

And soon to be compulsed to revert
From where they get distracted earlier by dint of a
flickery glance on her
The harshest reality here posing a deterrent
Against their's beholding to the most prettiest
creature of God...

Isn't it a paradox of our most cruel reality
One wants to get looked at, while the beholder
Of her is in a frenzy to get a glimpse at the
slightest pretext
Thus the forever mutual attraction of opposite
sexes
Acted upon as an impetus and stimulant to
Human beings' continuous journey to upkeep the
sustainability and enshrined civilisation...

Pathway's Autobiography...

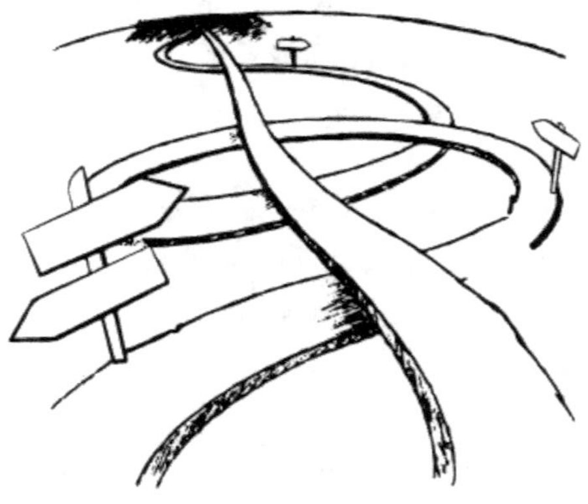

I am your repository of conveyance
By dint of which you can ply on me
To reach various destinations as per the need
Anyone who goes outside can return home
By following a definite path of myself...

The people often use me as and when needed
Without bothering a bit or due caring
I get rubbed, squeezed and often overloaded
Resulting in my indiscriminate damages
Which often leads to potholes, subsidence and
even wiped out partially...

My immense forbearance and
Propensity to take the maximum burden
Arising out on any type of road journey
Always has become completely selfless
At the altar of all others' interest
Whosoever plying on me...

Isn't it the magnanimity per se, then what
Wouldn't I have had the wherewithal
To expect something reciprocal
From my users also...

Otherwise, I will go for my last journey bit by bit
By losing every prospect of revival
With this unfortunate dying down of myself
A long legacy, a repository of proceedings and a
bouquet of memories
Will go down to oblivion once and for all...

Our life...

Life is precious for all
We live for our life
Everyone sought the meaning of life
But de facto fruition is elusive for most of us...

But shouldn't we continue our journey
Of course, we should
Life is always a roller coaster ride
Accompanied by headwinds and tailwinds...

Here every stage of life
Pertains to different purposes and perspectives
Sometimes gaining precedence by inlaid
weightage
Or get subdued by not so compliances...

At your sound mind, physique and earnings
You are the unassailable king of your own fiefdom
But with their decaying, you gradually will lose
the plot
Arising out dependability may bridle your so-far
charted terrain...

The journey of life is like an evolving flower
It gets blossomed, achieves completion and drops
to the ground finally
In between, it disburses beauty, essence and
rejoicing
And finally loses its identity at the very ground of
Mother Earth

www.ingramcontent.com/pod-product-compliance
Lightning Source LLC
LaVergne TN
LVHW011034200726
843509LV00011B/1281

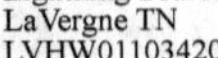